THE BRITISH FLORIDAS & THE AMERICAN REVOLUTION

WHEN shots were fired at Lexington and Concord on April 19, 1775, Great Britain's imperial territories in North America and the Caribbean consisted of 33 colonies, stretching from Nova Scotia in the frigid North Atlantic to Grenada in the southernmost waters of the Caribbean. When the distance between the capitals of these two colonies is measured you find East Florida, with the only set of stone fortresses south of the Chesapeake Bay, firmly anchored at the geographic center of the British Americas, and set squarely between the valuable sugar islands of the Caribbean and the rebellion.

It's a surprise for most people to learn that there were more than 13 British colonies when the American Revolution broke out. The "13 original colonies" are praised in songs and tributes across the nation. But inside what are now the borders of the continental United States there were actually 15 British colonies. As a nation, we tend to forget that with the 1763 Treaty of Paris that ended the French and Indian War there were vast amounts of territory across the Americas awarded to Great Britain's growing empire. Within the present-day United States this included the Spanish colony of Florida, which the British divided into two colonies because of its size, and added to the North American Bureau of the Colonial Office. When East Florida and West Florida were written into the colonial records their order was simply determined alphabetically since they were brought into the empire at the same time. For far too long East Florida and West Florida have been considered unimportant to Revolutionary War events, but nothing could be further from the truth.

FROM SPAIN TO BRITAIN

In August 1762, British troops captured Havana, Cuba, an important Spanish stronghold in the Caribbean and the capital of their most profitable sugar colony. In order to regain Havana, Spain traded the entire region of Florida to Britain as part of the 1763 Treaty of Paris. After dividing Florida into two colonies, the British kept St. Augustine as the capital of East Florida, while Pensacola would be the new capital over the colony of West Florida. Basically, East Florida was the present-day peninsula of Florida and West Florida was the panhandle of Florida and the bottom halves of Alabama, Mississippi, and Louisiana up to the Mississippi River.

Hudson's Bay

L. Superior

R. Missouri

R. St. Lawrence

Quebec

Montreal

C. Breton I.

Louisburg

Acadia

Champlain

New England

Crown Point

Oswego

L. Huron

L. Michigan

F. Niagara

L. Ontario

L. Erie

Ticonderoga

Boston

Nova Scotia

Pennsylvania

Fort Duquesne

New York

R. Ohio

Philadelphia

Alleghany Mts.

Virginia

R. Mississippi

Chesapeake Bay

Georgia

Bermudas ::

New Orleans

W. Florida

E. Florida

Rio Grande del Norte

GULF OF MEXICO

C. Sable

Bahama Is.

Tropic of Cancer

MEXICO

Campeachy Bay

Mexico

Cuba

Santiago

G. of Honduras

Jamaica

Porto Rico

St Eustatius

Hayti I.

St. Christopher

Antigua

Nevis

Guadeloupe

Dominica

Martinique

St. Lucia

St. Vincent

Grenada ★ Tobago

Trinidad

CARIBBEAN SEA

Cartagena

Porto Bello

R. Orinoco

SOUTH AMERICA

ATLANTIC OCEAN

EASTERN &
CENTRAL
AMERICA
1763

British
French
Spanish
Dutch

English Miles

— 3 —

WHY ST. AUGUSTINE WAS SO IMPORTANT TO GREAT BRITAIN

WHILE the story of the 13 colonies has always been the heartbeat of the birth of the United States, Great Britain had bigger concerns — protecting the priceless sugar-producing colonies of the West Indies from French, Spanish, and Dutch invasion. In the 18th century, sugar had the same impact on world economics as crude oil does today. The production of sugar and the system of slave labor that produced it were so profitable that European empires became dependent upon sugar and its by-products of rum and molasses to finance their visions of global expansion.

The southern colonies of Virginia, North Carolina, South Carolina, and Georgia were the agricultural heart and soul of British North America; East Florida and West Florida struggled economically until after the Revolution began. With British planters in the Caribbean dedicating as much as 98% of the soil on some islands to sugar production, the southern colonies of North America were needed to supply the British West Indies with food, flax and cotton for clothing, barrel staves, and naval stores such as pine tar, pitch, turpentine, timber, etc. Most plantation

West Indian Sugar Mill

BARREL STAVES
For All Your Needs!

Barrel staves are the long, narrow slats of wood curved to form the sides of barrels, which were used as shipping containers for practically everything in the 18th century.

Curved Strip of Wood

owners in the West Indies wouldn't have been able to feed or clothe themselves or their slave populations without these agricultural products from the southern colonies. Nor would the West Indies have had the capability to repair fishing boats or cargo ships transporting sugar products to Britain.

When the royal governors of Virginia, the Carolinas, and Georgia fled their capitals in fear of their lives, the plantations of the British West Indies lost their source of much-needed goods produced in North America. The only two southern colonies that remained loyal to King George III were East Florida and West Florida. In fact, once news of the Declaration of Independence reached St. Augustine, an angry crowd gathered in the city plaza on August 11, 1776, and hung effigies of Samuel Adams and John Hancock before setting fire to them.

The threat of having valuable North American agricultural supplies cut off by the new Continental Congress was a serious concern to Parliament. A series of counterstrikes were devised in the fall and early winter of 1775, calling for the British military, Loyalist militias, and all Native American allies in the region to reclaim the southern colonies.

St. Augustine residents outraged by the Declaration of Independence

Britain was preparing to launch what would become the first of two major invasions into the southern colonies. Striking out from positions in Pensacola, the Georgia and South Carolina backcountries, the Cape Fear River in North Carolina, St. Augustine, and New York – even as far as Ireland in the British Isles – the offensive would proceed in stages. The first stage began on August 12, 1775, with an order from General Thomas Gage, commander of all British troops in North America, for Native Americans in the southern frontier regions to attack all disloyal colonists. On October 16, King George III authorized a full-scale military invasion of the South, christening it the "Southern Expedition." The first attack fleet was to set sail from Ireland for the Cape Fear River on December 1, 1775, under the command of the Earl, Charles Lord Cornwallis.

The southern colonies were vital to British military strategies for squashing the rebellion because of the economic base they held in the production of food stuffs and flax that fed and clothed the slave population in the West Indies – and St. Augustine played a major role in those plans. Never forget the importance of sugar production to the profits of Great Britain in the 18th century. As a result, East Florida was so important to Britain's war effort that George Washington mentions St. Augustine in over 80 letters to the Continental Congress or his general staff as either a military target or a military concern. And the British fully understood the importance of keeping St. Augustine safe for king and country, which was why on March 1, 1774, they installed a career military man as the new governor. His name was Lt. Colonel Patrick Tonyn.

THE "14TH COLONY"
MYSTIQUE

Everyone understands that there were 13 original British colonies that unified to form the United States. But many people take the term "original colonies" to mean that there were no others - a total of 13. That's not only incorrect, but as a result the existence of a 14th colony takes on an almost mythological quality, like finding Atlantis or the Holy Grail. And it makes a great book title!

The truth is that colonies weren't added numerically - it was always by date. With Caribbean islands shuffling between European empires like an enormous shell game or Three Card Monte after each war, altering a colony's numerical placement every time it changed hands would have been nonsense. But for those who still insist that assigning a number to each colony is important, just remember that Nova Scotia was awarded to Britain in 1713 by the Treaty of Utrecht. This would make them the 11th colony, followed by North Carolina, South Carolina, and Georgia - the 14th colony.

Oops!

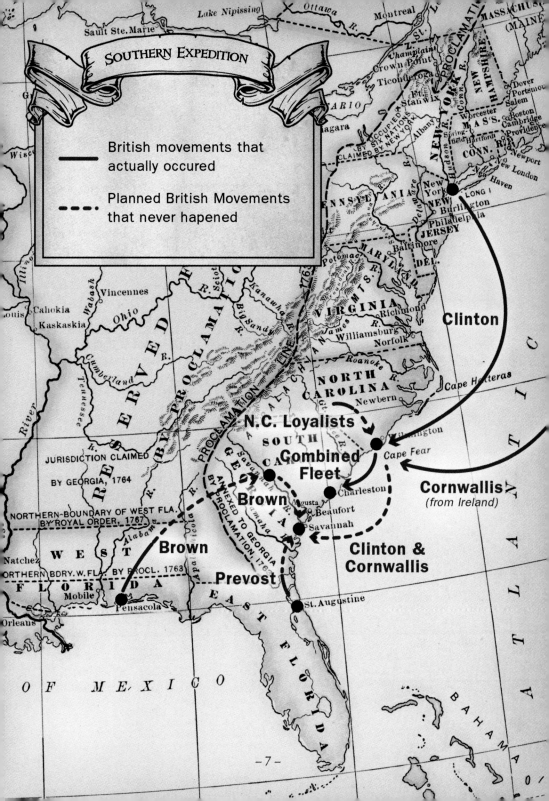

Upon his arrival in St. Augustine, Governor Tonyn put the garrison to work improving the defenses of the city. Guns were added and the palisades fortified at the large 17th-century masonry fortress on the northern end of the city (today the fort is under the care of the National Parks Service and the name has been returned to its original Spanish origins: the Castillo de San Marcos). Though Governor Tonyn owned 20,000 acres just north of St. Augustine, he had never been in East Florida. Imagine his delight once he saw the Castillo and realized what a military jewel he was inheriting. Tonyn made the refurbishment of the Castillo one of his top priorities, as well as the Spanish-built lines of defense that stretched across the northern approaches to the city gate.

Building the earthworks around St. Augustine

Tonyn also ordered the completion of the unfinished earthworks and redoubts around the perimeter of the city. Each plantation was required to provide 10% of their slave force to perform the work. New barracks were erected at the south end of town to replace the ramshackled quarters that were in place when he arrived. Being a career military man, Tonyn understood the sense of pride and honor that such a facility would give the troops. St. Augustine would not only seem a bit more comfortable now, but the British soldiers would know that the new governor was "one of them."

But even without these additional defensive efforts, the fact that St. Augustine was built on a peninsula made invasion by land from any compass-point but north extremely difficult. Additional defensive

Historic cannons may still be seen today on the walls of the Castillo de San Marcos "guarding" the St. Augustine harbor from ancient foes.

structures included small outposts further south on the St. Johns River (due west of St. Augustine), built to warn of western approaches. Fourteen miles south of the city, where the Matanzas River again meets the Atlantic Ocean, sits a second Spanish-built stone structure, Fort Matanzas. This smaller fort was designed to hinder any attempt by incoming enemy warships to approach the city from its "backdoor." Governor Tonyn had a firm grasp on the military significance of his colony, but so did George Washington. And just as Congress ordered an invasion of Canada in mid-1775 to remove any threats against the nation's northern borders, the same was true with their concerns of British threats stemming out of East Florida and West Florida. Before the American Revolution was over, Washington would authorize five separate invasions of East Florida from 1776 – 1780.

FORT MATANZAS

Fort Matanzas is the smaller of the Spanish-built masonry forts in the area and protected St. Augustine's southern approach from the sea. Inspired by a British attack in 1740, construction on the fort began later that year and was completed in 1742. The fort was named for the river that flows lazily past its gun ports. But in 1565, this was the site of a French massacre at the hands of Spanish troops under Don Pedro Menendez de Aviles, the founder of St. Augustine. In Spanish, *Matanzas* means "slaughters." Today, the fort belongs to the National Parks Service and is free to visitors.

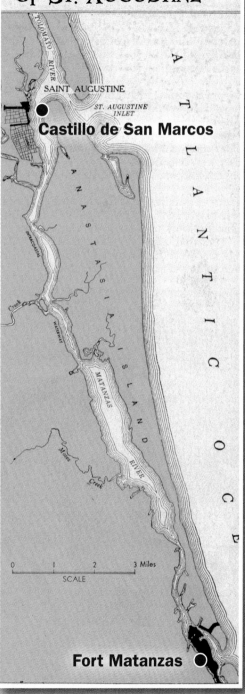

MASONRY FORTS OF ST. AUGUSTINE

Castillo de San Marcos

Fort Matanzas

Invading East Florida Was No Easy Task

In a letter to American general William Moultrie, Colonel Charles Cotesworth Pinkney described marches into East Florida in this way: "One campaign to the southward is more fatiguing than five to the northward." But an invading army had few options to work with, and all led to the same point on the map. The deadly Okefenokee Swamp and the eastern Creek borderlands created a barrier against entering East Florida from Georgia by land from any direction but north. The unforgiving terrain of South Georgia funneled armies into the region between the swamp and the Atlantic Ocean on the King's Road, the best entrance into East Florida, before fording the difficult St. Marys River. At

Fighting in the swamps of East Florida was a brutal business.

its narrowest and most obvious crossing point, the river was safeguarded by British troops stationed at Fort Tonyn.

Once in East Florida, an army would have to leave the King's Road or be exposed, forcing it into smaller swamps even closer to the ocean. These lands

Swampland such as this was nearly impossible to cross with cannon and gear.

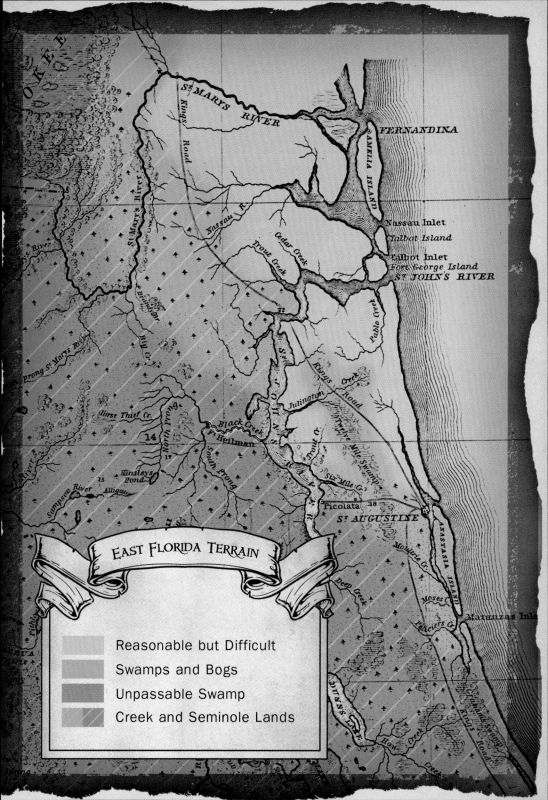

EAST FLORIDA TERRAIN

Reasonable but Difficult
Swamps and Bogs
Unpassable Swamp
Creek and Seminole Lands

River while dealing with another British outpost. If that was accomplished, the weary troops were funneled once again even closer to the Atlantic Ocean as they marched past the "12 Mile Swamp." From there they would wade through the unprotected marshes and estuaries of the coastal flood

were a quagmire of quicksand, biting insects, disease-carrying mosquitoes, alligators, poisonous snakes, panthers, black bears, and stagnant, brackish water. After slugging their way through nearly 40 miles of muck, the Americans would then need to cross the wide and powerful St. Johns

19th-century woodcut of a Florida swamp

FORT MOSE

Gracia Real de Santa Teresa de Mose (Fort Mose) was the first free black settlement in what is now the United States. Established in 1738 by Governor Manuel de Montiano to assist slaves fleeing British plantations in the Carolinas and Georgia, Fort Mose would become a rallying point during the British invasion of 1740 by General James Oglethorpe. After evacuating to St. Augustine, the Spanish army - led by Fort Mose's black militia - drove the British from their land in a resounding victory.

plains and smaller creeks, soon to become target practice for the sharpshooters of Fort Mose, located just two miles north of St. Augustine. If they could successfully muscle their way past that point, the invaders would complete their tortuous journey by having no choice but to march out of the bogs and straight into cannon fire from the revamped Spanish-built Cubo Line, which was stationed just in front of the heavily fortified Castillo de San Marcos. If Washington had received better information about the terrain of East Florida he might not have been so anxious to send his armies into such a place.

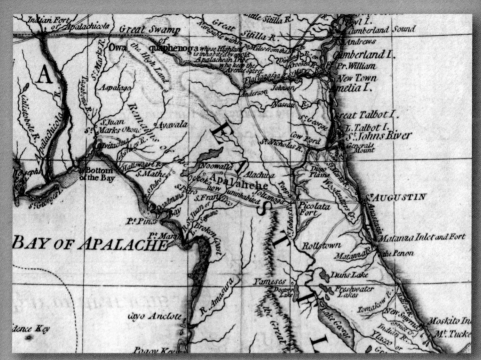

Section of map published in 1776 by Bernard Romans showing the coastal regions of south Georgia down to New Smyrna, and west to the border of West Florida.

An invading army's view of the Castillo de San Marcos and the Cubo Line

LT. COLONEL THOMAS BROWN ...

Thomas Brown came to Georgia in September 1774 with 29 indentured servants and a 5,600-acre grant of land located 30 miles north of Augusta. The great-grandson of Sir Isaac Newton and son of a wealthy shipping magnate, Brown was a die-hard Loyalist and not shy about it. On August 2, 1775, about 100 Sons of Liberty came to the home where Brown was staying and demanded he sign an oath of loyalty to the independence movement or take a thrashing. Brown scolded those who would claim to stand for liberty while demanding that he sacrifice his own freedom of choice in the process. About half of the men felt shamed and left. Brown slipped into the house, while the rest of the mob pressed onto the porch. He returned, brandishing pistols and a sword, but the fight was brief. Brown got off one shot that found its target but was struck with a rifle butt, fracturing his skull. He was then taken back to Augusta where the Sons beat him, stripped him down to his boots, and tied him to a tree. Before it was over Thomas Brown was scalped three times, then tarred and feathered; his legs were badly scalded as the tar collected in his boots. The Sons pulled off his boots and put hot brands to his feet, burning off two toes. Brown was then tossed into an open cart and paraded from one end of Augusta to the other. The Georgia Gazette mockingly reported Brown's torture as his "being presented with a genteel and fashionable suit of tar and feathers," and the Sons of Liberty would tag him with the nickname of "Burnfoot Brown." They would soon regret this day.

... AND THE EAST FLORIDA RANGERS

When Governor Patrick Tonyn arrived in St. Augustine he ordered the colony's defenses improved and repaired. As rebellion swept the southern colonies, more and more rugged, backcountry woodsmen and farmers brought their families to East Florida for the protection of the king's troops. Tonyn saw this as an opportunity to build an army of men who knew well the landscapes of Georgia and the Carolinas and how to fight while living off of the land. Tonyn had the men – what he didn't have was the right man to lead them, and this was becoming a concern. But in December 1775, a fully recovered, seething Thomas Brown came to St. Augustine and was introduced to Governor Tonyn. Tonyn had his man. Brown was extremely intelligent, respected as an aristocrat, tough enough to handle the rigors of guerilla warfare, and very angry. The Rangers knew how to fight and how to survive in the country, but Brown taught them the art of espionage and the importance of gathering reliable information from rebel nerve-centers. He taught them the strategy and tactics of lightning-strike raids. Most importantly, he taught them to set aside their differences with the allied Native Americans and to utilize the skills they brought to this type of combat. General Augustine Prevost would incorporate the Rangers into the regular army and rely upon Thomas Brown heavily in the campaign to re-claim Georgia in 1778. In 1779, the Rangers held their position with distinction as Prevost's troops withstood an allied French/American attempt to re-take Savannah.

Collection of the Fort Ticonderoga Museum.

THE INVASION OF 1776

O N December 17, 1775, General
Washington was handed a packet
of stolen letters informing
him that Great Britain was stockpiling
arms and ammunition in St. Augustine.
From this information Washington
believed that the British would launch
an invasion into the southern colonies

GEN. CHARLES LEE

Passing stolen information.

from East Florida. On January 1, 1776,
Congress resolved "That the seizing and
securing the barracks and castle of St.
Augustine will greatly contribute to the
safety of these colonies, therefore, it is
earnestly recommended to the colonies
of South Carolina, North Carolina and
Georgia to undertake the reduction of
St. Augustine." Washington authorized
General Charles Lee, second in command
only to Washington himself, to march on
East Florida with a combined army of
militias from the three states mentioned
by Congress, along with regiments of the
Southern Department of the Continental
Army from Virginia, North Carolina, and
South Carolina. In all, Lee's army totaled
2,500 men. The conquest of East Florida

was extremely important for several reasons, not the least of which was the valuable war supplies held in the fortress in St. Augustine. But the Castillo itself may have been the greatest prize of all. By capturing St. Augustine, the Continental Army would gain a historically invincible position, leaving nothing but saltwater between American borders and European armies in the West Indies.

In mid-January 1776, Congress sent Representative John Rutledge of South Carolina to oversee the formation of a new American government in St. Augustine, as well as to inventory the captured war supplies. Imagine Rutledge's shock when on February 13, his journey to St. Augustine was stopped short in Charleston. Rutledge was fully expecting to find American patriots in the South Carolina capital celebrating an American victory in East Florida. Instead, he learned that General Lee had not begun the assault. Due to Lee's lack of enthusiasm for Washington's orders (marches into the alligator and disease-infested swamps of East Florida were dangerous and costly), Lee was recalled to Charleston. General Robert Howe assumed Lee's command and posted the army in a defensive position in Savannah. He would not leave for East Florida until Lee rejoined him on August 19 — nine months after Washington's urgent request to Congress.

Meanwhile, in East Florida, advanced British regulars and militia began arriving on the banks of the St. Marys River on the Georgia–East Florida border as early as May 29. Knowing nothing of a possible American invasion, Prevost was awaiting orders to march into Georgia as the southern flank of the Southern

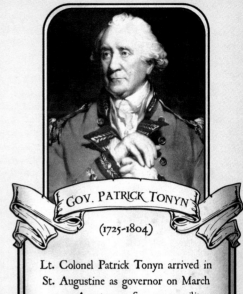

GOV. PATRICK TONYN

(1725-1804)

Lt. Colonel Patrick Tonyn arrived in St. Augustine as governor on March 1, 1774. A veteran of 33 years military service as a dragoon, Tonyn earned merit and promotions in the Seven Years War. His assignment to East Florida was simple: keep the colony secure from the rebellious activities brewing to the north. But East Florida's elites were almost all Scots, who resented an Irishman as governor of their colony. As a result, Tonyn's battles more often than not involved political attacks rather than American invasions. East Florida remained loyal throughout the war and on November 13, 1785, Major General Patrick Tonyn would be the last royal governor to evacuate North America.

Expedition. But Cornwallis's fleet from Ireland had been scattered across the Atlantic by a hurricane, keeping the entire British invasion of the South hopelessly off schedule. By late June, companies of

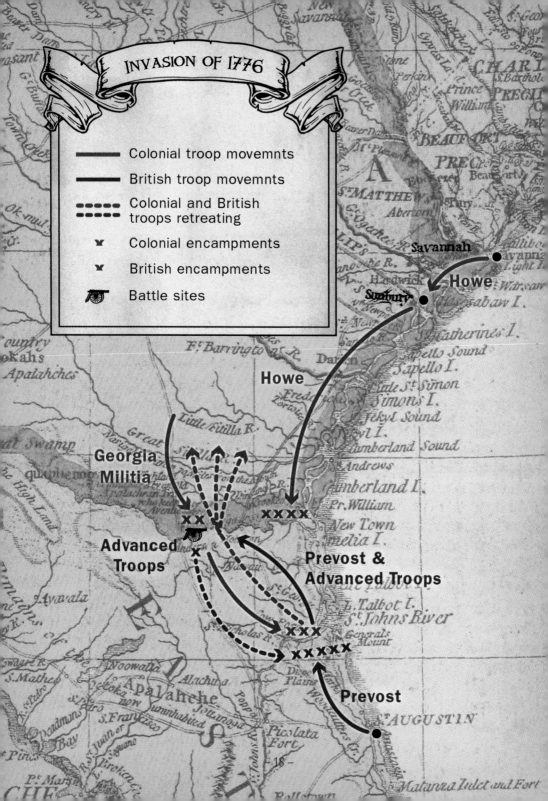

INVASION OF 1776

——	Colonial troop movemnts
——	British troop movemnts
▬▬▬	Colonial and British troops retreating
⚔	Colonial encampments
⚔	British encampments
🎯	Battle sites

Savannah

Howe

Sunbury

Howe

Georgia Militia

Advanced Troops

Prevost & Advanced Troops

Prevost

ST AUGUSTIN

Smoke from the next farm down!

Georgia militia steadily built up along the northern banks of the St. Marys River. Border skirmishes broke out, and by late July the Georgians had crossed into East Florida and were holding a sizable portion of the colony. The northern border of East Florida was now the southern banks of the St. Johns River.

As the main body of the Continental Army reached Sunbury, Georgia, three days march from the St. Marys River, there was an outbreak of multiple fevers in the camp. The army was ravaged by the time it reached the East Florida border, losing as many as 15 men a day from a combination of yellow fever and malaria. With his army too weak to continue, General Howe was forced to halt his approach. Meanwhile, the Georgia militia – still holding the ground between the St. Marys and St. Johns rivers – found a new threat against which they also had no defense: rumors of Cherokee war parties attacking along the Georgia frontier. The Americans lost no time retreating back into Georgia to protect their homes and families. As Governor Tonyn wrote, "The Americans are a thousand times more in dread of the [Indians] than of any European troops." Historians often scoff at the idea of southern Native Americans playing a large role in the British war effort, but those men who fought in the South understood that mere rumors were enough to turn entire armies about-face. Lieutenant Walter Scott of the Loyalist Refugees noted, "The talk of their [Cherokee] going to war has certainly answered a very good intention by keeping a great many Rebels upon the Frontier which greatly helped the [British] troops by keeping so many men from them." Frustrated, Washington recalled General Howe, ending the first invasion of East Florida.

THE INVASION OF 1777

WASHINGTON had not given up on securing East Florida and the war supplies being stored in St. Augustine. In the late campaigns of 1776, the commander-in-chief had requested from Congress 30,000 flints and several tons of powder, and these needs were only growing worse as the war progressed. Gaining such a large cache of supplies being storehoused in St. Augustine would not only strengthen the resources of the Continental Army, but deplete those of the British in equal measure. But this was only one of the general's obsessions with the region. Even more critical was the Castillo itself. Built of coquina, a unique rock formation found in only a few other locations around the Caribbean, the fortress had never fallen to an invading army (and never would!) due to its superior design and materials, as well as a plentiful supply of fresh water. Completed in 1695, the Spanish architects even found a way to utilize the tides to "flush" the fort's latrines twice a day. Amply supplied, the Castillo had withstood sieges lasting as long as three months or more. With such a battle-tested fortress already built and functioning, Washington could control the destinies of the southern colonies with much greater ease of mind.

In the spring of 1777, Washington ordered a second invasion of East Florida, giving command of approximately 1,200 Georgia militia and Continental regulars from Virginia and Georgia to Brigadier

THE WONDER OF COQUINA!

It wasn't uncommon for forts of the Revolutionary era to be constructed of wood and highly susceptible to fire and dry rot. Not surprisingly, confidence among colonists for these structures ran low. Though masonry fortresses did exist in North America, they were few and far between. But what made the forts of St. Augustine like no others on the continent was that they were quarried from the local coquina pits on Anastasia Island. Coquina is not a rock formation in the traditional sense of the term. It forms from millions of tiny, compressed, decaying seashells and the lime they secrete rather than from mineral compounds like other stone substances. Because of its porousness, coquina can breathe in the summer and insulate in the winter, but most importantly, coquina can absorb the kinetic shock of an 18th-century cannonball! The British were all too familiar with this neat little trick from the many failed assaults on St. Augustine since the Castillo was completed in 1695. Many were the British artillerymen who had been confounded by the wondrous nature of coquina.

General Lachlan McIntosh. But this arrangement nearly doomed the campaign before it began. Button Gwinnett, a signer of the Declaration of Independence, Georgia's second governor, and current militia leader was furious that McIntosh, his long-time political rival, was placed in such a position over him. Insults and hostilities between the two leaders quickly spread to the junior officers and ultimately through the ranks. The situation became so inflamed that before the army could enter East Florida, McIntosh and Gwinnett were recalled to Savannah. This left the American army without strong leadership on the eve of the invasion. McIntosh denounced Gwinnett before the Georgia Council of Safety as a liar and one of "dangerous ambition." Outraged, Gwinnett challenged McIntosh to a duel. While both men were hit by the exchange

The duel between General McIntosh and Button Gwinnett

of gunfire, McIntosh survived his wounds. Gwinnett would die just days later. The expedition, now under the command of Lt. Colonel Samuel Elbert, crossed into

How many names do you recognize on the Declaration of Independence?

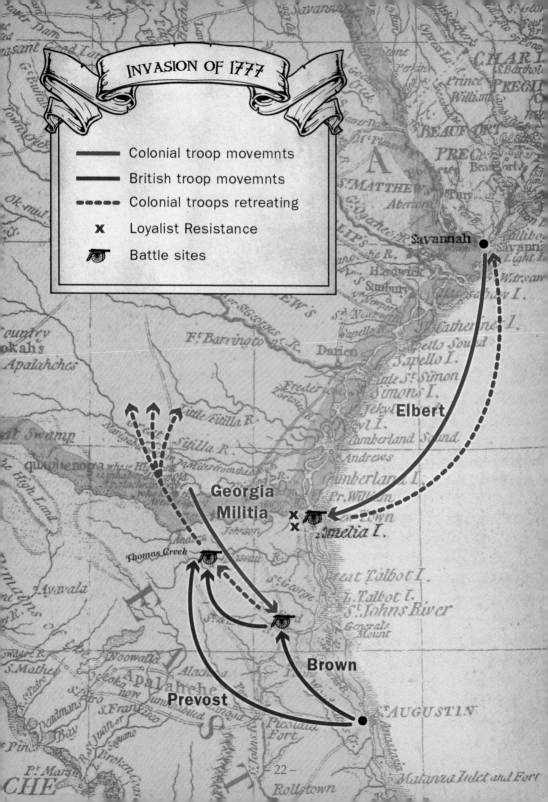

INVASION OF 1777

————	Colonial troop movemnts
————	British troop movemnts
●●●●	Colonial troops retreating
x	Loyalist Resistance
🔫	Battle sites

Savannah

Elbert

Georgia
Militia

x
x

Thomas Creek

Brown

Prevost

ST AUGUSTIN

East Florida at Oldtown Bluff on the north end of Amelia island. After securing the island they were to move onto the mainland and rendezvous with Colonel John Baker's Georgia light horse dragoons near the St. Johns River. However, Baker's unit was intercepted by Thomas Brown's East Florida Rangers and Indian allies and driven back to Thomas Creek. There

Burning Governor Tonyn's property

Baker met a company of British regulars under Major Mark Prevost (General Prevost's brother) and was decisively defeated. Though Baker escaped, Elbert's invasion plans that Baker carried were dropped as he fled, making any thoughts of continuing the invasion as originally designed pointless. Meanwhile, Elbert's ships were unable to cross the shallow waters between Amelia Island and the mainland. A skirmish with Loyalists on Amelia Island forced Elbert to reconsider

the invasion altogether. He withdrew his troops to Savannah by sea, but not before ordering many of the houses burned and cattle killed in retaliation for losing one of his officers in the fight.

At one critical point when Baker's Georgians were gaining ground, General Prevost recommended a scorched-earth policy to keep outlying plantations from providing food and shelter to the invading American army. One of the plantations that Prevost reported as threatened was that of Governor Tonyn. As a career military man, Tonyn fully understood what had to be done. The governor ordered his entire 20,000-acre plantation burned to the ground. This meant the destruction of two large manor houses, over two dozen outlying barns, buildings, quarters, and mills, along with all of the agriculture in the fields and in storage and all of the timber on the property. What was once an extremely large and valuable estate was now nothing more than smoldering ruins. As fate would have it, the invading army was turned back long before reaching his plantation, so it was all for naught, though it certainly demonstrated the governor's resolve to keep his colony secure for the Crown. Tonyn would begin the rebuilding process as soon as the colony's borders were once again safe, but he was presently without a home, and the Government House where he conducted the affairs of the colony didn't offer the best of circumstances for a family of six. Lt. Governor John Moultrie would come to the Tonyn family's aid by offering the Moultrie town-home in St. Augustine, where they would live until the evacuation of the colony in 1785. You can see the house today on St. George Street. Known as the Peña-Peck House, it has been in the care of the Woman's Exchange of St. Augustine since 1931.

Peña-Peck House

to retain ownership of their plantations once the colony was taken. Penman went so far as to declare that if Tonyn did not agree to their demands, then he would ignore the governor completely and meet the oncoming army by himself with a flag of truce to make his own arrangements. Needless to say, this is not the kind of demand one should make to a governor (or anyone else) who just destroyed his own valuable plantation and all of his possessions in order to frustrate the invading American army. When the smoke cleared and the second invasion was but a bad memory,

But that's not to say that every Loyalist in East Florida had the same passion for king and country. As Baker's Georgia dragoons gained steam after piercing the first of the British defenses on the St. Marys River, three so-called Loyalists – Spencer Mann, James Penman, and Lt. Colonel Robert Bissett – came to Governor Tonyn demanding their right to surrender to the invading Americans. The three even proposed to pay the rebels a great deal of money if their properties went undamaged and they were allowed

Government House

the humiliation that followed these three men plagued them for the rest of their days in East Florida.

Before the end of 1777, Spencer Mann would be called upon by Governor Tonyn to witness and sign the depositions of

19 Menorcan indentured servants who accused Dr. Andrew Turnbull (founder of New Smyrna plantation, bitter enemy of Tonyn's, and close colleague of Spencer Mann) of extreme physical and legal abuses. Tonyn would shut down New Smyrna plantation, giving Dr. Turnbull's financial investors in London no other option but to sue him for their losses. James Penman, Spencer Mann, and the entire Turnbull family would be forced to escape to Charleston in 1780, just prior to the British siege of that city. Lt. Colonel Bissett, being an officer in the British army, was in complete disgrace.

Taking depositions

THE SONS OF LIBERTY IN EAST FLORIDA?

Typically we think of the Sons of Liberty as a New England-based movement with chapters in the large cities and towns of the American colonies. But when the Stamp Tax Crisis of 1765 rocked the British colonies, rioting mobs were found as far south as Nevis and St. Kitts in the British West Indies. In East Florida there was no such movement in 1765, because the colony was still in its infancy in the British Empire. But on February 27, 1776, seventy-four men attended a clandestine meeting in St. Augustine at Woods Tavern on Artillery Street (the present-day site of the Episcopal Church's thrift store). Governor Tonyn would accuse their leaders of treason and conspiracy against the Crown, calling them a "cabal of dissensionists and agitators."

Chief Justice William H. Drayton and Secretary of the Colony Dr. Andrew Turnbull were the most prominent names noted. Others were James Penman and Spencer Mann, as well as Lt. Colonel Robert Bissett and Lt. Colonel Lewis Fuser of the British army, and the colony's attorney general, Arthur Gordon. Tonyn had little patience for politics, much less factions created for the sole purpose of stirring up trouble. The governor risked losing his office on several occasions to rid East Florida of these men. Innocence or guilt wasn't as important to Tonyn's investigations as was simple obnoxiousness. To those he disliked most, Tonyn became a vindictive tyrant, and many on this list would flee to Charleston in 1780 in order to escape his wrath.

THE FIRST INVASION OF 1778

I N April 1778, Washington authorized a third invasion of East Florida, once again sending a combined army of Continental regulars under the command of General Robert Howe and Georgia militia under the leadership of Governor John Houstoun – approximately 2,000 troops in all. The Americans initially breached British border defenses by land, but not the complex system of waterways leading indirectly from the St. Marys River to St. Augustine. According to some historians, the American invasion of 1778 was turned back by nothing more than a rumor that five heavily armed British gunboats were patrolling the St. Johns River. But there was certainly more than loose gossip involved in the defense of the colony.

Militia and Rangers fighting from behind earthwork defenses.

Captain John Mowbray of the *Rebecca* and other privateers defended East Florida's waterways, sailing under Letters of Marque issued by Governor Tonyn. Attacking St. Augustine by sea was virtually impossible in the colonial era. St. Augustine's shallow inlet from the Atlantic Ocean into the city's harbor was notorious during the age of wind and sail because of a continuously shifting sand bar at the inlet. The "Crazy Banks," as they became known, forced any ship with a draft of over 7–10 feet (a ship's draft is the distance from a ship's waterline to the lowest part of the vessel) to remain at sea. Therefore, ships-of-the-line, frigates, and other large fighting ships could hardly approach the bar, much less pass over it. The smaller craft that could cross the bar became cannon fodder for artillery crews in the Castillo. Bringing an army down on St. Augustine by land was more practical, but incredibly difficult. The only true Achilles' heel in protecting St. Augustine from invasions was the difficult system of river ways.

PRIVATEER OR PIRATE

Privateers were not pirates. Privateers were captains (and their crews) who owned their own vessels and were provided a "letter of marque" by a king or other official, such as the governor of a colony, to legally wage war against foreign ships on the high seas. A classic example of privateering during the American Revolution is the entire U.S. Navy. The nation didn't own a single ship and relied upon privateers such as John Paul Jones. Pirates were quite often privateers whose letters of marque were no longer valid or who had decided to go into business for themselves.

Waging war at sea

In late June, while Mowbray and his fresh-water navy watched over the hundreds of miles of estuaries, creeks, bays, and tributaries of the colony's two major rivers, Lt. Colonel Thomas Brown and a small party of East Florida Rangers and allied Creek Indians sat guard at Fort Tonyn on the St. Marys River to provide first-strike warning of American attacks by land from Georgia. But once again, in-fighting over command of the American army threatened to sink the campaign before it began. General Howe ordered an attack on Brown's Rangers at Fort Tonyn before advancing on St. Augustine, while Houstoun insisted on bypassing Brown and marching directly on the capital. Tempers flared so hotly that Houstoun refused to cross into East Florida. What none of the Americans knew was that Thomas Brown had sent spies into Georgia and South Carolina, and was tracking the army's movements. While Houstoun sat, Howe sent an advance company of 100 mounted dragoons under General James Screven and Colonel Elisha Clark across the St. Marys River to attack Fort Tonyn, but Brown put the fort to the torch and retreated. As Screven's dragoons gave chase, General Howe brought the main body of the Continental Army into East Florida. Houstoun sat.

There was some light skirmishing as Screven and Clark pursued Brown, but the Loyalists always remained just far enough ahead to keep contact to a minimum. Brown's Rangers and allied Creek warriors were familiar with the

This illustration of the Battle of Cowpens demonstrates the type of fighting between Brown and Screven.

landscape and well-acclimated to the heat and humidity. After a 17-mile chase under impossible conditions, Screven's forces ran face-first into Major Mark Prevost's British regulars and more East Florida Rangers at Alligator Creek Bridge. The Americans would find out all too late that Brown's retreat had been calculated to keep Screven in hot pursuit. Just before reaching Alligator Creek, Brown's troops had peeled off to each side of the only road available and lay in wait to close the trap. Some escaped the ambush and slowly met up with the main body of Howe's regulars, but by this time the army was out of food, exhausted, and bloodied. Swamp fevers and disease sent the Americans back to the St. Marys River. After Howe made several appeals, Houstoun finally crossed into East Florida on July 6 to relieve what was left of the continental units – about 400 men capable of bearing arms. Incredibly, divisions over command would begin immediately, due to Howe's failure. The Americans had no choice but to retreat across the St. Marys River on July 14, as Howe and Houstoun began to prepare their contradicting reports to Congress.

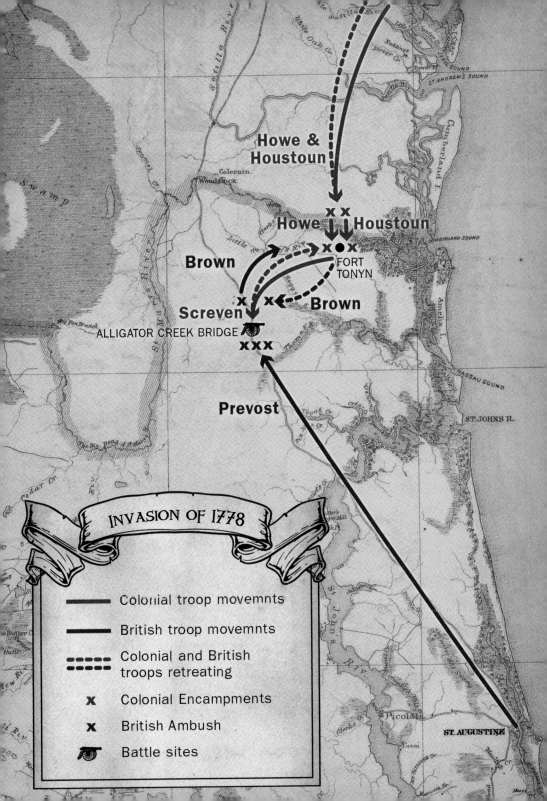

Howe &
Houstoun

Howe ✗ ✗ Houstoun

Brown ✗ ✗
FORT
TONYN

✗ ✗ Brown
Screven

ALLIGATOR CREEK BRIDGE

✗✗✗

Prevost

INVASION OF 1778

—— Colonial troop movemnts

—— British troop movemnts

- - - Colonial and British
troops retreating

✗ Colonial Encampments

✗ British Ambush

🔫 Battle sites

ST. AUGUSTINE

The Second Invasion of 1778

Even after the dismal results of Howe's most recent attempt to take East Florida, Washington ordered a second campaign for 1778 to take place as quickly as possible, for time was against him. His network of spies on Long Island, now known as the Culper Ring, produced reliable information showing that British troops amassed in New York were staging for simultaneous strikes against Savannah, St. Lucia in the West Indies, and the Mississippi Delta. A 5,000-man British army left New York for St. Lucia – the only gain in the Caribbean that Britain would claim for the entire war, while another 3,500 troops sailed from New York to St. Augustine. There, 2,500 men disembarked and the remaining 1,000 sailed for Pensacola, via Jamaica. Washington wanted to take East Florida before the massive British offensive could get under way, but his valued French

le Cte De Rochambeau

> ## The Myth of Saratoga
>
> While it is true that the British surrender at Saratoga on October 17, 1777, brought France into the war, it was not the reason that Britain campaigned in the southern colonies from 1778-1781. These orders were issued on September 3, 1777 - six weeks before Britain's defeat at Saratoga.

military advisor, General Jean-Baptiste Donatien, comte de Rochambeau, convinced Washington that there wasn't enough time to put together another southern offensive. What Rochambeau may have been too polite to say was that, given the southern army's history for in-fighting, another march into East Florida could just be a repeat of the last. Rochambeau's advice was taken and the southern army was sent to bolster General Howe's defenses of Savannah. But General Prevost would bring 2,500 British troops up from St. Augustine to rendezvous with the fleet out of New York under Lt. Colonel Archibald Campbell. Savannah fell easily and most of Howe's 5,000-man army was taken prisoner. Georgia was once again British.

THE INVASION OF 1780

IN 1780, Washington would once again cast his eye on the prize of St. Augustine and the idea of sweeping the British army into the sea. Even with the loss of Georgia in December 1778, and the failed attempt to re-take Savannah by a 10,000-man French and American allied army in the fall of 1779, Washington issued another all-out offensive against East Florida. But again, General Rochambeau would advise against it, believing that it was a mistake to deploy so many valuable troops on another foray into East Florida when British general Cornwallis was tromping northward through the Carolinas toward Virginia. As much as Washington wanted to see an American flag flying over the ramparts of the Castillo de San Marcos, he agreed that Cornwallis must be dealt with first. Ultimately, it was Cornwallis's ego that would be his undoing. The goal was for him to pacify the area between Charleston and the Chesapeake Bay, where he and General Clinton would deliver the death blow to the rebellion. But Cornwallis was concerned that Clinton would arrive first and take all the glory. In his haste, Cornwallis pacified nothing and arrived at Yorktown too early...and was trapped.

THE WAR IN THE WEST

The war for the western regions is almost as invisible in our history books as the five invasions of East Florida. The Spanish were not as concerned with Britain's military might in West Florida - it was the illegal smuggling between British traders and Spanish merchants that was cutting deeply into the Spanish colonial treasury. But in 1778, Britain sent 500 provincial regulars from Maryland and 500 German Waldeckers to Pensacola. The idea was to attack New Orleans at the same time that General Prevost and Lt. Colonel Campbell bore down on Savannah. In addition, Major Patrick Sinclair was to march from Fort Michilimackinac in upper Michigan to attack the fort at present-day St. Louis. The goal was to encircle the southern colonies by claiming the length of the Mississippi Valley, the Gulf Coast, and the Atlantic seaboard. But the 500 troops from Maryland picked up small pox when their ships re-supplied in Jamaica. By the time they reached Pensacola the mortality rate of those sick was nearly 50% and the survivors were too ill to disembark. Sinclair was soundly defeated by Spanish militia and an American unit under George Rogers Clark.

CONCLUSION

As the American Revolution came to an end, East Florida would be the only British colony south of the Canadian border to never lower the "Union Jack." West Florida, with its deep harbors on the Gulf Coast, lush forests, and the rich soil of the Mississippi Valley, was taken by Spanish forces from New Orleans and Havana in a series of campaigns and major battles from 1779 – 1781. From the fall of Pensacola to the end of the war, East Florida stood alone. But at the 1783 Treaty of Paris that ended the war, the British government gave East Florida back to Spain for the sake of keeping their fort on Gibraltar. Gibraltar guarded the narrow entrance into the Mediterranean Sea and the vast wealth offered in its markets and trade routes.

Many of the 21,000+ people in East Florida – the majority being replanted Loyalists from fallen southern colonies – felt betrayed. Former Rangers, captains Daniel and James McGirtt, formed an outlaw gang immediately after hearing the results of the treaty, as did many British regulars who would desert to join the McGirtts or form gangs of their own rather than ship-out to the West Indies.

On July 12, 1784, the new Spanish governor, General Vicente Manuel de Zéspedes, officially claimed the colony for Spain. But the British evacuation didn't go smoothly. Zéspedes quickly lost patience with the whole process, while British subjects found false hope in the delays. Tonyn and Zéspedes, who hated each other from the outset, would spend the next 16 months living too close to each other for comfort. King George III ordered Tonyn to be the last man to leave the colony, and until that time he was still the governor over all British "interests" in the colony. Tonyn interpreted these instructions to the farthest extent that he possibly could: that East Florida was still his colony! After 16 months of annoying Governor Zéspedes to the fullest extent, General Tonyn sailed from East Florida on November 13, 1785 – over two years after the Treaty of Paris.

The preliminary signing of the 1783 Treaty of Paris